The Trials by Opera

of

Gilbert and Sullivan

and

Richard D'Oyly Carte

A PLAY IN TWO ACTS

Written by Jean Gouldsmith Skinner, Linda Barker, Miles Bailey

Copyright © 2019-2022 Jean Gouldsmith Skinner, Linda Barker, Miles Bailey

All rights reserved. No part of this publication may be reproduced or transmitted in any form or by any means, electronic or mechanical including photocopying, recording or any information storage or retrieval system, without prior permission in writing from the publishers.

The right of Jean Gouldsmith Skinner, Linda Barker and Miles Bailey to be identified as the authors of this work has been asserted by them in accordance with the Copyright, Designs and Patents Act 1988

First published in Great Britain 2022
by The Choir Press

ISBN 978-1-78963-144-9

Performance Rights

This work is protected by copyright and a fee must be paid for each performance.

All performance enquiries should be made to the publisher at:

The Choir Press,

132 Bristol Road, Gloucester GL1 5SR

enquiries@thechoirpress.co.uk

PRODUCTION NOTE

The authors envisage that the music in this production may be provided either by recordings or live performance.

Contents

Introduction		1
Cast in order of appearance		3
Scene 1	Trial by jury, January 1875	4
Scene 2	The birth of their first success, January 1875	13
Scene 3	Helen Lenoir – the peacemaker, June 1877	15
Scene 4	Grossmith gossips, May 1878	20
Scene 5	Buying time, August 1878	25
Scene 6	Carte plays a card, April 1879	27
Scene 7	The investors' revolt, May 1879	31
Scene 8	Causing a scene at the Opera Comique, July 1879	33
Scene 9	The winter of discontent, February 1880	35
Scene 10	Back home to Pirates, March 1880	41
Scene 11	The Garrick Gentleman's Club, April 1880	45
Scene 12	Patience is a virtue, April 1881	47
Scene 13	Savoy small talk, October 1882	52
Scene 14	Princess Ida's final performance, October 1884	54
Scene 15	The Mikado: rehearsal and rebellion, March 1885	56
Scene 16	The carpet quarrel, December 1889	64
Scene 17	Finale	68

INTRODUCTION

The phrase 'artistic difficulties' might have been coined to describe the working relationship between William Gilbert, Arthur Sullivan and Richard D'Oyly Carte. In 1875, Gilbert, a successful playwright and theatre critic, began to collaborate with Sullivan, the most famous composer in England, at the suggestion of the impresario Richard D'Oyly Carte.

Gilbert was a driven, assertive exponent of his topsy-turvy world, creating comic operas which poked fun at the class system, weaving stories around the likes of fairies, lord high executioners and pirates, all whilst appealing to Victorian standards of conduct and mawkishness. He brooked no interference in the staging of their work, demanding lavish sets, the highest standards of acting and singing, and elaborate costumes. Gilbert fumed at Sullivan's sybaritic lifestyle, believing it affected his partner's health and encouraged his dilatory production of the music needed for their comic operas. At the same time he fully appreciated the quality and originality of the music that Sullivan composed.

Sullivan, the beloved composer of 'The Lost Chord' and 'Onward Christian Soldiers', was determined to be taken seriously and not just remembered for light comic work. He fretted with dissatisfaction and made frequent pleas to Gilbert to change direction from fantastic plots, believing his own talents were being wasted. Aware of his temper and appetite for litigation, he nevertheless recognised and applauded Gilbert's undoubted flair and vision for their productions. Sullivan was feted by royalty and high society.

Unlike Gilbert, he didn't marry, but was a dedicated and popular ladies' man.

Richard D'Oyly Carte was the first of the opera impresarios. Recognising that their combined talents could produce stunning work, he encouraged Gilbert and Sullivan to work together, resulting in a new genre which had immediate and great appeal for Victorian England. Whereas previously visits to the musical hall theatre had been amidst large and rowdy crowds in noisy and extremely hot atmospheres, their works attracted a better-behaved clientele where women could attend with confidence to enjoy the shows unpestered, unbothered and in comfort. Carte built his own theatre at the Savoy and introduced the first electric lighting to the theatre, as well as a form of air conditioning. Carte was a canny and sometimes ruthless and rapacious businessman, but his assistant, Helen Lenoir (later the second Mrs Richard D'Oyly Carte), was his invaluable, gentler right hand, smoothing squabbles and efficiently organising contracts and travel arrangements. Everyone was devoted to her.

The authors of 'The Trials by Opera of Gilbert, Sullivan and D'Oyly Carte' have imagined scenes between these protagonists based on extensive research – luckily a wealth of information is readily available about their intriguing lives – the result being a play in two acts for performance with live or recorded music.

Cast in order of appearance

Lucy Gilbert, aged 28	William Gilbert's wife
William S. Gilbert, aged 39	Librettist
Judge	High Court judge
Bridie O'Riley	Irish defendant
Mrs Briggs	Defendant (non-speaking)
Police Constable	Cockney policeman
Gallery	Chorus
Prosecuting Counsel	Barrister
Clerk of the Court	Clerk of the court
Maid	Arthur Sullivan's housemaid
Arthur Sullivan, aged 45	Composer
Richard D'Oyly Carte, aged 30	Talent agent and impresario
Helen Lenoir, aged 25	Business manager for Richard D'Oyly Carte
George Grossmith, aged 31	Actor and singer (baritone)
Singer	An aspiring singer
Jessie Bond, aged 25	Singer and actress (mezzo soprano)
George Metzler	Co-founder and investor in the Comic Opera Company
Augustus Collard Drake	Co-founder and investor in the Comic Opera Company
Thugs	Hired by the investors in the Comedy Opera Company
Stage Crew	At the Opera Comique theatre
Waiter	At the Garrick Gentleman's Club
Frederic Clay, aged 42	Composer and friend of Arthur Sullivan
Rutland Barrington, aged 28	Actor and singer (baritone)
Sybil Grey, aged 25	Actress and singer (soprano)
Leonora Braham, aged 32	Actress and singer (soprano)
1st, 2nd and 3rd Character	Cast members from The Mikado
Richard Temple, aged 39	Singer (baritone)

The ages of the main characters are given in respect of the first scene in which the character appears.

Scene 1

Trial by Jury, January 1875

Part I

Lucy is seated at small breakfast table. Gilbert enters looking tired and dishevelled in his dressing gown.

Lucy	William, what on earth is wrong? You look a sight.
Gilbert	Oh my dear, I have had the most frightful night of repeated and demoralising humiliations! I'm exhausted!
Lucy	Sit down and tell me. What do you mean?
Gilbert	It's this wretched 'Trial by Jury' manuscript! I'm afraid it's given rise to some bad dreams and rather ugly memories of my disastrous days at the Bar!
Lucy	But that was years ago, William.
Gilbert	I know, but the idea of being back in the courtroom still haunts me. *(Lights fading.)*

Part II

Lights down on the morning room scene. Curtains open, Gilbert removes his dressing gown and walks into a lit-up court scene. Dreamy music and smoke effects.

Stage set with Judge's bench, dock, witness box, counsel bench and gallery.

The novice Gilbert enters the courtroom in an agitated and nervous manner and stands next to prosecuting counsel. He fumbles with his papers anxiously, notices some of the Haymarket Theatre Company in the gallery and gives a worried wave.

Prosecuting Cnsl.	First night nerves, Counsel? Still pursuing your legal career and

	dabbling in the theatre, eh, Gilbert?
Gilbert	You observe correctly, sir, and I rather rashly invited the Haymarket touring company to witness the proceedings! No doubt you are aware, Counsel, of my theatrical aspirations and one is casting one's net you understand.
Usher	All rise.

The courtroom rises. Judge enters in comic, doddery fashion.

Start of 'The Judge's Song' to be performed amongst the courtroom players in a spritely yet elderly style.

Judge	When I, good friends, was called to the Bar.
	I'd an appetite fresh and hearty,
	But I was, as many young barristers are,
	An impecunious party
	I'd a swallow-tailed coat of a beautiful blue –
	A brief which I bought off a booby –
	A couple of shirts, and a collar or two,
	and a ring that looked like a ruby.
CHORUS	He'd a couple of shirts, and a collar or two,
	and a ring that looked like a ruby.
Judge	At Westminster Hall I danc'd a dance
	Like a semi-despondent fury
	For I tho't I never should hit on a chance
	Of addressing a British jury
	But I soon got tired of third-class journeys
	And dinners of bread and water
	So I fell in love with a rich attorney's
	Elderly, ugly daughter.
CHORUS	So he fell in love with a rich attorney's
	Elderly, ugly daughter.

Judge	The rich attorney, he jump'd with joy
	And replied to my fond professions,
	'You shall reap the reward of your pluck, my boy
	At the Bailey and Middlesex sessions
	You'll soon get used to her looks,' said he
	'And a very nice girl you will find her.
	She may very well pass for forty-three
	In the dusk, with a light behind her.'
CHORUS	She has often been taken for forty-three
	In the dusk, with a light behind her.
Judge	The rich attorney was good as his word
	The briefs came trooping gaily
	And every day my voice was heard
	At the sessions of ancient Bailey.
	All thieves, who could my fees afford
	Relied on my orations
	And many a burglar I've restored
	To his friends and his relations.
CHORUS	And many a burglar he's restored
	To his friends and his relations.
Judge	For now I'm a judge
	And a good judge, too,
	Yes, now I'm a judge
	And a good judge, too,
	Though all my law be fudge
	Yet I'll never, never budge
	And I'll live and die a judge
	And a good judge too.

Judge sits down very satisfied with his performance and everyone sits.

Usher	Bring in the accused, Bridie Dymphna Francis O'Riley.

An old weather-beaten and rough Irishwoman enters and stands in the dock and gives her oath ... I swear ...

Gilbert	*(Stands)* You are charged, Mrs O'Riley, with stealing a coat on the ...
Bridie	Ah will yer sit down, yer divil ... Don't listen te 'im, Yer Honner! He's known in all the slums of Liverpool –
Gilbert	*(Interrupts)* Mrs O'Riley, please ...
Bridie	Ah sit down, yer spalpeen! He's as drunk as a lord, Yer Honner, begging Your Lordship's pardon.

The Judge and the court are falling about laughing.

Gilbert	Ahem! You were arrested, Mrs O'Riley, by Constable Glum after being seen ...
Bridie	Ah what does he know! He was away with the fairies on the night in question, Yer Honner. Well there, yer only have to look at his faisog to see he's too fond of the ole grog!
Gilbert	Madam, please! Constable Glum is an officer of the law and as such ...
Bridie	Between you, me and the gatepost, Yer Honner, he's a sodden sop of a baggage and has such is hunworthy of hundertaking his solemn duties and that's the end if it!
Gilbert	Your Honour ... will you not reprimand this woman and bring her to order ... I am supposed to be defending the vociferous wretch!

Everyone in court by now is howling with laughter, whilst the accused looks haughty with her nose in the air.

Judge	Hmmm ... Pity, Counsel, we were all enjoying the spectacle! *(Bangs his gavel.)*
	Three month's detention at Her Majesty's pleasure, Mrs O'Riley, and

	you can attribute my leniency to some spirited entertainment value. Next case!

Bridie is escorted out, remonstrating with the Usher.

Muttering and chuckling in the courtroom as court adjourns temporarily awaiting next case.

Usher	Call Mary Elspeth Briggs.

A prim-looking woman dressed in black with a white collar and a puritan hat enters dock and takes oath.

Usher	You stand accused of picking the pocket of a fellow omnibus passenger Mrs Edwina Smythe.
Gilbert	I call witness Constable Freeman.

Constable enters and swears oath.

Gilbert	Constable Freeman. I'm sure that you can save the court's time and bring this matter to a swift close by relating the circumstances of this alleged crime.
Constable	Yes, sir.
Gilbert	You are aware that the accused was travelling on the afternoon in question to a tea and prayer meeting at the time of the alleged incident?
Constable	Oi am, sir.
Gilbert	And the fact that the accused always carries a hymn book in the very pocket in which the stolen purse is alleged to have been located?
Constable	Oi am, sir.
Gilbert	And, therefore, we can safely assume that the most likely circumstance is that the said pocketed purse was indeed planted on the accused in the hope of extorting some remuneration from the

	devout Mrs Briggs.
	Now you said you found the purse in her pocket, my man?
Constable	Yes sir.
Gilbert	And did you find anything else?
Constable	Yes sir.
Gilbert	What?
Constable	*Retrieves his notebook from his breast pocket licks his pencil, locates his notes.*
	Two ovver purses, a watch wiv' a broken bow, free han'kerchiefs, two silver pencil cases and … *(Looks up)* a 'ymn book.
	Roars of laughter from the court and exhibits on a tray shown to the jury by the court Usher.
Gilbert	You may stand down, Constable
	He starts to sit down in despair.
	Call witnesses to Mrs Briggs's character.
Usher	Call witnesses to Mrs Brigg's character.
Usher	Call witnesses to Mrs Briggs's character.
	No one appears, more muttering, the perplexed Usher looks for direction from Gilbert.
Gilbert	*(Stands)* Begging Your Lordship's pardon. It is really most unfortunate, they must have mistaken the day.
Prosecuting Cnsl.	Shouldn't wonder!
Judge	*(Bangs his gavel)* Eighteen months' hard labour!
	Mrs Briggs stoops down, pulls off a heavy boot and flings it at Gilbert

uttering a stream of invective. The boot misses Gilbert and hits a reporter in the gallery, whom we see making fierce notes after he has recovered from the blow.

The court explodes with laughter.

Judge	*(Bangs gavel again)* **Court adjourned.**
Usher	All rise.

The court disassembles, quietly singing 'The Judge's Song' through a smoky atmosphere and fading away. Gilbert and the Prosecuting Counsel stand up and gather their papers.

Gilbert   I fear it doesn't bode well for this profession, for which I had high hopes and invested the £400 left to me by my aunt.

The two start to walk out together.

Prosecuting Cnsl.   I think you'll make more money from your satirical writing in Byron's *Fun* magazine, William. Your work has a wicked, acerbic quality.

Gilbert   Mark Lemon at *Punch* refused my 'Yarn of the Nancy Bell' on the grounds that it was too cannibalistic! He said that feeding off the blood of others was not to the taste of his readers! Hah!

Prosecuting Cnsl.   Irreverent maybe, and vindictive towards those who abuse their power perhaps, but never malicious and always humorous.

Just what we expect from a full-blooded and belligerent Englishman such as your good self! Hey! Mark Lemon will go down in history as a joke! You give us just the right amount of propriety whilst relieving us of the burden of prudery with a good hearty belly laugh!

Gilbert   Very well if you say so, old chap … I do enjoy the battle between daring and discretion, indeed everything that is topsy-turvy! But I don't like to be vilified.

Prosecuting Cnsl.   Then don't poke fun at the establishment, William!

Prosecuting Counsel exits as Gilbert dons his dressing gown and moves back into the breakfast room scene with his wife Lucy through smoky atmosphere. He sits down at the breakfast table again.

Part III

Lucy: William! William!

Lucy gently prods him and he suddenly becomes aware of his surroundings.

I was just saying, dear, that was years ago.

Gilbert: Oh yes ... yes ... *(Coming to his senses)* Yes it was, but hey-ho, my time at the Bar has given me some rather useful fodder for this libretto that Richard D'Oyly Carte has asked me to share with Arthur Sullivan.

Lucy: D'Oyly Carte! How did you meet him?

Gilbert: Oh, I just bumped into him by chance on my way out of the Garrick last week.

Lucy: I didn't know you knew him.

Gilbert: Well I don't, but everyone knows who he is, and anyway, he knew who I was, and before I knew where I was I was telling him about this libretto I'd written and he was telling me that he thought Arthur Sullivan and I would make a rather successful alliance and I was telling him ...

Lucy: I seem to recall that your first collaboration with Arthur Sullivan was not exactly a resounding success. Are you sure you want to –

Gilbert: If you're referring to 'Thespis' Lucy, then yes it was ... hmm .... disappointing. Rather more operatic extravaganza than opera comique. 'Trial by Jury' on the other hand is satirical in essence and besides, four years has passed since then.

Lucy: ... and didn't you say that you'd asked Carl Rosa to write the music

	for it? I hope you're not letting him down. He's just lost his wife, poor man.
Gilbert	Of course not, dear! I'm afraid poor Carl is still reeling from the death of his wife and he returned the manuscript, and so when Carte thought it had possibilities he arranged …
Lucy	So he's read it already?
Gilbert	He does have something of a reputation for spotting winners you know.
Lucy	Oh well if you think …
Gilbert	Yes, dear, I do! And he's arranged a meeting between Sullivan and myself this morning *(Gets up from chair with renewed vigour).*
Lucy	What, in this filthy weather? … I just don't want you to be disappointed.
Gilbert	No time like the present dear … *(Kisses her forehead and leaves.)*

Suggested music: 'Hark The Hour Of Ten' is sounding.

Scene 2

The birth of their first success, January 1875

Maid knocks on the breakfast room door and enters.

Maid	Mr Gilbert for you sir.
Sullivan	Gilbert! Good to see you.

Maid takes coat.

Gilbert Sullivan.

Sullivan I wasn't sure that you would venture out on such a filthy morning.

Gilbert Oh … er … well you know … *(Rather flustered)* can't let such trifles get in the way of making progress … such as it is … and I have er … I have recently dramatised this story originally written for *Fun* magazine and Carl Rosa was to write the music but after his wife died, he couldn't face it. Then Carte got involved … and well you know him, he can talk his way … well anyway … here we are.

Hands the manuscript to Sullivan.

Carte has read it and thinks it's got possibilities so here I am … though I'm really not convinced it's up to the mark you know. I have grave doubts and … well, libretti in general … you know I'm just not sure.

Sullivan Well don't keep me in suspense, Gilbert. Let's hear it!

Gilbert It's a one-act spoof of the British courtroom, ahem … of which I have had some rather painful experience myself … at the Bar you understand, not in the dock! A jilted bride-to-be sues her former fiancé for breach of contract resulting in a ludicrous trial where any ideals of romance are eclipsed by the realities of greed and lust!

	Added to which the characters behave as if the events are all perfectly reasonable. Carte wants it as a companion piece for Offenbach's 'La Perichole'!
Sullivan	Oh indeed? I am a great admirer of Offenbach's work.
Gilbert	Hmmm … Well shall we begin?

Lights down. A little of 'The Judge's Song'. Lights up. Sullivan laughing.

Gilbert	I was trying to use a narrative style that, at one and the same time, has the sharpness of pointed barbs and yet is acceptable to the paying public. It's aimed, you see, at the hypocrisy of those in authority and the base motives of supposedly respectable people and institutions.

A moment's silence, Sullivan looks down. Gilbert looks a little nervous.

Sullivan	It's hilarious! I refuse to countenance your reservations. I can't wait to get started … leave it with me and I'll make a start.
Gilbert	Oh, er very well then, if you think you can do something with it. *(Prepares to leave)* When shall I hear from you?
Sullivan	*(Rings the bell)* All in good time Gilbert … all in good time. *(Maid enters)* Mr Gilbert is just leaving, Maud, kindly see him out.
Maid	Yes of course, sir.
Gilbert	Until I hear from you then, Sullivan.
Sullivan	Soon, Gilbert. Soon.
Sullivan	Oh and Gilbert. I think I have just the person for the Judge … My brother Frederick.
Gilbert	Hmmm. Good day.
Sullivan	Good day.

Suggested music: a few bars from 'Oh Joy Unbounded'.

Scene 3

Helen Lenoir – the peacemaker, June 1877

Richard D'Oyly Carte's office.

Carte   Arthur Sullivan will be here shortly to discuss the final terms for our next production. It's called 'The Sorcerer'. Gilbert has already outlined the story to me. This will be our first full-length comic opera and the start of a new era.

Helen   I admire your enthusiasm. *(Pause)* But have your investors agreed to this piece? 'Trial by Jury' was only one act. I know it was very successful but a full-length opera is a much bigger challenge and a lot more expensive to stage.

Carte   They'll agree to it … I'm sure they will.

Helen   Really? Are you sure these investors won't be more trouble than they're worth?

Carte   Helen, I need their investment to pay the production costs. I simply don't have the capital to do this on my own. Anyway, they value my knowledge and experience.

Helen   And the talents of William Gilbert and Arthur Sullivan.

Carte   Yes, yes of course Gilbert and Sullivan … *(Excitedly)* but Helen, this agreement *(Waves document)* with George Metzler and Augustus Drake to form the Comedy Opera Company is probably the most important business arrangement I shall ever make and it will change the course of my business. It will also change the course of musical theatre in this country, if not the world.

Helen   But all that glitters is not gold. Mr Gilbert and Mr Sullivan are undoubtedly talented but they are not … how shall I put it …

	straightforward.
Carte	*(Defensive)* What do you mean?
Helen	Gilbert turns people away from him with his overbearing attitude.
Carte	Well maybe.
Helen	There's no maybe about it, Henrietta Hodson, John Hare, Henry Labouchere, William Kendall – all respected theatrical friends of his who won't speak to him now. He's even fallen out with his mother. Sullivan on the other hand is popular … I hear that perhaps he is a little *too popular* in some quarters and he has so many requests for his work that he can be unreliable.
Carte	All business involves risk.
Helen	That's true, but you've persuaded four wealthy businessmen to invest in this Comedy Opera Company. These investors will have high expectations and you will be under a lot of pressure to make Gilbert and Sullivan deliver the results. And you haven't got a contract with them yet.
Carte	It's a recipe for success. I'm sure of it. The Comedy Opera Company has been set up specifically to bring a new type of musical theatre to London – performances that a respectable man could take his wife to.
Helen	Yes, all of them written and directed by Gilbert and Sullivan. But do you have any other writers or composers who could create this new musical theatre?
Carte	Well … er … no. I'm sure there are others who could do something similar … maybe.
Helen	Hmmmm. I'm not so sure about that. I was reading your agreement with the Comedy Opera Company last night. They'll take a big portion

	of your profit.
Carte	But I don't *have* the capital to do it on my own. I have to take the risk.
Helen	You already have one of the most successful agencies – your clients are among the most sought-after artists and performers in London. But this business with Mr Gilbert and Mr Sullivan could expose you to risks you can't quantify.
Carte	Now you sound like a mathematician.
Helen	*(Laughing)* I am a mathematician.

Pause and a brief smile and look between them that might just infer there's a little more between them than purely a business relationship.

Knock on the door. Enter Arthur Sullivan.

Carte	Sullivan, good to see you. May I offer you a tea, or something a little stronger perhaps?
Sullivan	*(Jovial)* No, no thank you, Carte, I'm under doctor's orders – no tea or coffee for a while.
Carte	This is my assistant, Miss Helen Lenoir. She has a natural gift for business planning and organisation … usually of me.
Sullivan	I'm delighted to meet you, Miss Lenoir.
Helen	I'm delighted to meet you Mr Sullivan. It's not every day one meets such a celebrated composer.
Sullivan	You flatter me, madam.
Helen	I think not, sir. *Onward Christian Soldiers* and *The Lost Chord* are exceptional pieces of music.
Sullivan	The success of *The Lost Chord* is bittersweet. It was written in the hours of despair at my brother's bedside as I watched him slipping away. It's true that my music has been popular. But the success has

	also given weight to those critics who would discourage me from writing comic opera. In some corners of the press anything less than an orchestral opus is perceived as cheap and unworthy.
Carte	This is a musical and theatrical revolution and you will be leading it. They'll be eating their words soon.
Sullivan	Let's hope their indigestion is not reflected in the reviews we get.
Carte	Miss Lenoir and I have been discussing your proposals to produce *The Sorcerer* to open later this year. You asked for 200 guineas in advance, which we're willing to agree to, and six guineas for each performance.
Sullivan	That's correct and not at all unreasonable.
Carte	That's an advance on only the first … er … thirty performances.
Helen	Well thirty-four actually.
Carte	That's an advance on only the first thirty-four performances. I'm optimistic we'll achieve at least 150, maybe 200.
Helen	And we'd like to have the piece ready to start rehearsals on 29th August this year. I believe Mr Gilbert has already written the libretto.
Sullivan	*(Sullivan is uncomfortable and Carte looks surprised)* That's much sooner than I had anticipated. I'm about to go to Paris for three weeks and I haven't composed any of the music yet.
Carte	How long will it take?
Sullivan	It's difficult to say, but 29th August gives me less than twelve weeks and that's not quite long enough …
Helen	Splendid, so another month should see it done. Let's agree on 29th September.
Sullivan	Er well … I … I'm not sure … um … yes … yes alright, 29th September.

Carte	Well that's settled then. I'll prepare contracts for you and Gilbert to sign.
Sullivan	Right! Well I shall be seeing Gilbert today and I'll let him know we've agreed the terms. Good day, Miss Lenoir, Carte.
Carte and Miss L	Good day.

Exit Sullivan.

Carte	Well that went very well, but I didn't realise you were planning to start rehearsals on 29th August.
Helen	I'm not. But it was the only way Sullivan would agree to start by 29th September.
Carte	Oh I see.
Helen	Richard, if anything goes wrong with this, you will be the filling in a very messy sandwich between the investors of the Comedy Opera Company and Gilbert and Sullivan.

Carte puts his hands across his face in a thoughtful manner.

Scene 4

Grossmith gossips, May 1878

Suggested music: 'Never Mind The Why and Wherefore'.

Scene is a theatre dressing room. George Grossmith is seated, writing. A singer enters (could be male or female).

Grossmith	Can I help you?
Singer	I'm here to audition for the satire.
Grossmith	You'll never get the part if Mr Gilbert or Mr Sullivan hear you calling it a satire, my dear! *(Theatrically)* We perform OPERA! COMIC OPERA!
Singer	Oh, I see, yes, that could have been disastrous. Actually, I don't know very much about the production at all except that it's called 'HMS Pinafore'. Could I possibly trouble you to tell me something of it?
Grossmith	There is nothing to tell. I have neither seen the lyrics nor heard the music.
Singer	I beg your pardon. I thought you were Mr Grossmith, Mr George Grossmith, the famous baritone singer of Mr D'Oyly Carte's Comedy Opera Company.
Grossmith	*(Sweeps a theatrical bow)* Indeed I am.
Singer	And the production opens in eight days' time?
Grossmith	Again, your information is impeccable!
Singer	I don't understand.
Grossmith	As we speak, child, Mr Sullivan is composing incomparable music for Mr Gilbert's reflections on the arbitrary nature of society's absurd rules and regulations. *(Noises of raised voices offstage, slamming of doors, etc.)* Or perhaps not. We see the score tomorrow.

Singer	That argument, it's not Mr Gilbert and Mr Sullivan is it?
Grossmith	Your accuracy really is quite impressive, my fair young person. I think I also decipher Mr D'Oyly Carte's sonorous tones and darling Miss Lenoir's soothing and tactful interventions. Today's falling out is, I believe, a business matter. Or it may be due to Mr Gilbert's artistic dominance, or Mr Sullivan's music not being allowed to 'rise and speak for itself', or, indeed, what to have for luncheon.
Singer	They argue frequently then, do they?
Grossmith	You have a lightning grasp of facts do you not, sweet child?
Singer	Erm, I think perhaps this position is not for me. If you'll excuse me I'll just make my way out, thank you for your help Mr Grossmith. *(Grossmith waves languidly and laughs to himself. Singer stops starstruck as Jessie Bond enters)* Oh, gosh, oh, I say, it is, isn't it? Oh, gosh … *(Stares enraptured at Jessie.)*
Grossmith	It is indeed the divine Miss Jessie Bond, mezzo soprano soubrette and darling of London audiences.

Singer, flustered and awkward, exits, muttering Great pleasure, miss, er, yes, indeed, er, excuse me, er. George and Jessie look at each other and laugh.

Jessie	Who was that, George?
Grossmith	Just a waif, or a stray, I'm not sure which. *(Nods to offstage)* How are they?
Jessie	Upset, and angry with each other. I dare say it will blow over, like it always does, but it's very unsettling for the company. Mr Gilbert is being dogmatic, Mr Sullivan is complaining about Mr Gilbert's attitude, Mr Carte is concerned with profit and Miss Lenoir is pouring oil on troubled waters.

Grossmith	As always. That woman is a saint. A brilliantly clever and pacifying saint.
Jessie	Why do they argue so much, George? They produce wonderful work together.
Grossmith	Where to start? Sullivan wants stories of human interest and probability. Gilbert sees a chaotic world – accidents of birth, fate and human blunder, confusion and delusion. A world where nobody is really who or what they seem to be. But they know how to write for each other.
Jessie	So why the constant arguments?
Grossmith	Sullivan is frustrated that, in his view, he never has time to write what he calls 'proper music'. He feels he's frittering away his life and talents on trivia.
Jessie	And Gilbert?
Grossmith	He's contemptuous of Sullivan's popularity and 'hobnobbing', as he calls it, with royalty and the aristocracy.
Jessie	I do find Mr Gilbert quite terrifying at times. He *is* intransigent and difficult to work for, but we all accept that because his artistic vision is so absolutely right.
Grossmith	Oh I agree, but I do think he underestimates Mr D'Oyly Carte's and Miss Lenoir's contributions. Mr Gilbert demands lavish (and expensive) productions and Mr Carte comes up with the theatres and the backers. And Miss Lenoir does the contracts, most of the casting, and looks after us all – a gargantuan task.
Jessie	Mr Sullivan is much easier, of course, warmer, kinder and quite charming. A trifle too charming with some married ladies! And perhaps a little pompous and swayed by celebrity and status. But, oh

	my goodness, it is nail biting waiting for his music. He leaves everything to the last minute.
Grossmith	And then we all struggle to learn the most complicated songs in rehearsal time that's been cut to the bare minimum.
Jessie	He does tend to get ill at critical times too.
Grossmith	And his womanising and partying don't help.
Jessie	One day, I fear, we'll miss an opening because Mr Sullivan, for one reason or another, just won't have finished the work in time.
Grossmith	And Mr Gilbert is the opposite, a diligent perfectionist, but then that's why we're so successful.
Jessie	He's not as approachable as Mr Sullivan.
Grossmith	But he is also a kind person – to animals! I once heard him say 'deer-stalking would be a very fine sport – if only the deer had guns!' *(Jessie laughs)* Seriously, he is a stickler but he's also very generous – as you know, Jessie – paying for cabs for all the girls to get home after late rehearsals and giving treats and gifts to all the children he comes across.
Jessie	He's not very kind to you, George. You get so nervous and it isn't just stage fright is it? *(George shakes his head)* You get in an awful state. In rehearsals, before and during the shows and *he* just makes things worse. I've seen you cry so many times after he's been bullying and hectoring you, and you're often very sick. I don't know how you carry on. *(George looks furtive and ashamed.)*
Grossmith	I take medicine, Jessie.
Jessie	I know, George. It's not a secret. Everyone knows.
Grossmith	Everyone?

Jessie	You're an addict George. That's difficult to hide. Look at Leonora Braham. We all know about her drinking, and we all know you inject morphine. *(George puts head in hands)* Mr D'Oyly Carte refused to renew Leonora's contract last year, but Mr Gilbert and Mr Sullivan must have persuaded him because she has just been re-engaged. So, George, I think you must be very careful about your own position here.

Suggested music: 'I'm Called Little Buttercup'.

Scene 5

Buying time, August 1878

George Metzler's office. Enter Carte.

Metzler	*(Agitated)* Ah yes, Carte, thank you for coming. I'll get straight to the point. You persuaded me and our other directors to invest in your Comedy Opera Company and we've supported you for two years. But my fellow investors and I are concerned that you simply aren't selling enough tickets for 'HMS Pinafore'.
Carte	But Metzler, it takes time to build a reputation with a new production. 'HMS Pinafore' is only our second full-length piece and we've had excellent reviews.
Metzler	We don't care about reviews. What we care about is the number of people who pay for tickets and there aren't enough of them. We're paying a fortune to lease the theatre, not to mention exorbitant wages for some of Mr Gilbert's 'preferred' performers.
Carte	We pay the rate for the artistes we need.
Metzler	Ar*tistes* eh! Damn it, Carte, I'm sure I could find *singers* for less.
Carte	I doubt it. Mr Gilbert is very specific about the characteristics of the people we hire.
Metzler	Is he indeed? Well, that brings me to another matter regarding Mr Gilbert. The set!
Carte	It's exceptional isn't it? Everyone praises it.
Metzler	But it was far more expensive than we anticipated. I was told that Mr Gilbert went to Portsmouth and made sketches on board HMS Victory, spent two days making a model and then insisted the

	theatre's carpenters built the set copying the model.
Carte	That seems very thorough and efficient, and the result is stunning.
Metzler	I've never heard of such a thing. It's not the way it's done and it's just not necessary. 'HMS Pinafore' is an opera. It is not part of Her Majesty's navy! The plain fact is that ticket sales are poor and money has been squandered which means … which means we cannot continue as we are.
Carte	Arthur Sullivan is already the nation's foremost composer. Don't throw that opportunity away now. The only reason ticket sales have been disappointing is because of the hot summer. The Opera Comique theatre is unpleasant when it's hot because there's no ventilation and the drains are smelly, but the weather's getting cooler now. Sales will pick up.
Metzler	I don't believe that! If you've had such good reviews and you're still not getting the sales in spite of Sullivan's reputation it proves to me the show isn't popular. I'm sorry but I'm going to have to recommend to the other investors that we close it as soon as possible.
Carte	But then you'll lose thousands of pounds that you've already invested. Do you *really* want to report that back to Augustus Drake and the other investors? If you back out now Mr Gilbert and Mr Sullivan will never work with you again, or more to the point, they might not work with me again. Give me two months. If it isn't making a handsome profit by the end of October – then you can close it.
Metzler	It's against my better judgement, but I'll give you until the end of September.

Scene 6

Carte plays a card, April 1879

George Metzler's office. Enter George Metzler and Augustus Drake.

Drake — I'm looking forward to seeing Carte again. I hope he's not going to be late – I'm having luncheon at the Criterion. I must say, George, it's been quite a turnaround hasn't it? When you reported to the investors last August I thought we were going to lose our money. What's happened?

Metzler — *(A little troubled by something as yet unexplained)* Carte and Sullivan used some of the music from 'HMS Pinafore' to hold promenade concerts at Covent Garden. It increased ticket sales so much that by the end of September, 'HMS Pinafore' was playing to full houses.

Drake — Clever eh!

Metzler — Carte has this idea he can transform musical theatre from its vulgar burlesque image. I mean to say – young women cavorting around half-dressed in their underwear.

Drake — Yes *(Enjoying the image he's conjuring in his head)*, yes indeed. Disgraceful, shocking.

Metzler — You couldn't take a respectable lady to that sort of thing, Drake.

Drake — I never do.

Metzler — Carte wants *his* productions to be suitable for the whole family and by doing so he thinks ticket sales will multiply. He seems to be on to something.

Drake — Well, as the chairman of the investors I must prepare a written report for our next meeting. I'll need some figures from you, Metzler.

Metzler	'Pinafore' is so popular there are now two touring companies in the provinces, and the piano score has sold thousands of copies.
Drake	Remarkable.
Metzler	Profitable.
Drake	Indubitable. *(Both laugh, but George is more subdued.)*
Metzler	*(Looks out of the window to the street below)* There is, however, a fly in the ointment of our success.
Drake	And that is?
Metzler	The fly has just crossed the street. He'll be here in a minute.
Drake	Aah I see. Carte himself – I might have guessed.
Metzler	He wrote to tell me there was an important matter he wanted to discuss. Something to do with the lease on the theatre.
Drake	Well damnation and blazes, Metzler, not another problem! The blasted theatre had to close for six weeks over Christmas for repairs to the drains or something. We make £500 a week out of this production, so we lost over £3000. Why isn't Carte able to find a decent theatre? That's his job isn't it?
Metzler	I don't think we can blame Carte for that – there are new health laws and the Ministry of Works insisted on the drain repairs.
Drake	Ministry of Works indeed. Pah! Interfering busybodies!

Enter Carte.

Metzler	Good morning, Carte. We were just discussing the unfortunate closure of the theatre last December. It was a rather expensive surprise.
Carte	Yes, it was most unfortunate, but there was nothing we could do about it. It's the new Public Health Act. But 'Pinafore' has been

	running again since the start of February.
Metzler	Plenty to look forward to then *(Looks at Drake and rubs his hands)*.
Carte	It was good while it lasted – but all good things come to an end.
Drake	What do you mean come to an end?
Carte	If you recall our contract, it says the Comedy Opera Company has the right to present 'HMS Pinafore' for the duration of the initial run.
Metzler	So what – it's now April and Pinafore is still playing to packed houses.
Carte	That, gentlemen, is because I was able to secure, on your behalf, a six month lease from 1st February until 31st July.
Drake	And what happens then?
Carte	What happens then is that because the closure in December brought the initial run to an end, Mr Gilbert and Mr Sullivan will have no further obligation to the Comedy Opera Company to allow it to perform 'HMS Pinafore'.
Metzler & Drake	*(Together)* What!
Drake	I don't know about Mr Gilbert, but I know for a fact that Mr Sullivan would never concoct this ruse to exclude us from what's rightfully ours. This is your doing isn't it, Carte? You extended the lease until July 31st to give yourself more time to plan your own production and cut us out.
Metzler	You can't expect us to risk our money in your theatrical productions and then just wave goodbye as soon as they start to show a profit. You should be more grateful to us for risking our money.
Carte	As I recall, last August you told me you were going to close the show because ticket sales weren't good enough. Naturally that made me realise I couldn't rely on your continued support. I persuaded you to

	keep 'Pinafore' running, as a result of which you've not only recouped your investment but made a very handsome profit. You should be grateful to me.
Metzler	That's a damned impertinence. It is you who should be grateful for the opportunity we've given you. And now that we've funded your production you think you can set up on your own and make money without us.
Carte	If you have a complaint you should discuss it with your lawyers who approved the contract.
Drake	There is such a thing as integrity in business, Carte, so you can rest assured the only conversation we'll be having with our lawyer is to expedite our claim against you.
Carte	I will of course defend it vigorously. Oh, and by the way, you may like to know that I have taken a new lease on the theatre from 1st August – in my own name.
Drake	Dammit, Carte! That's outrageous. We'll see you in court.
Metzler	By the time we've finished there won't be a theatre in London where you can perform your shows.
Carte	In that case, gentlemen, I shall just have to build my own!

Scene 7

The investors' revolt, May 1879

Enter George Metzler and Augustus Drake.

Drake	Have you seen this? *(Waves newspaper)* 'Pinafore' is playing to packed houses. The Evening Standard had a long piece about it last night. It makes my blood boil to think that at the end of July Carte is going to cut us out.
Metzler	He'll make a fortune.
Drake	We took the risk and he's going to reap the reward.
Metzler	*(Pause)* I've been thinking. Why don't we stage our own production of 'Pinafore'?
Drake	Can we do that? And what about actors? What about a theatre for God's sake?
Metzler	I've made provisional enquiries to hire the Imperial Theatre from 1st August, and some of the cast are willing to come over to us for a few shillings more each week.
Drake	But what about copyright? I've heard this copyright business is starting to be taken seriously by the courts, especially due to the efforts of the late Mr Charles Dickens.
Metzler	Carte is so busy in America trying to stop unauthorized productions over there that by the time he realises what's happening we'll be up and running.
Drake	If Carte sues for infringement of copyright, we'll counter claim for breach of contract and a share of all that profit he's making.
Metzler	That will muddy the waters for a bit.

Drake	He'll be making so much money that he'll have a lot more to lose than we have.
Metzler	We'll have at least six to nine months of argument and obfuscation … and by then we'll have a very healthy profit.
Drake	But what about the set? You have to have a set!
Metzler	We can hire some carpenters and build a set.
Drake	Hmmmm. I've got a better idea. We'll take it with us.
Metzler	What?
Drake	We'll take the set. The set that we paid for.
Metzler	You can't break into a theatre and steal a set.
Drake	We won't break in, we'll take it at the end of the performance on the last night and we're not stealing it, we're re-possessing it as the legal owners.
Metzler	I don't like the 'we' part.
Drake	Fear not, Metzler. It just so happens that I have some contacts in the world of … shall we say pugilism.
Metzler	Really, I never knew that.
Drake	Well it's … unofficial pugilism.
Metzler	Bare knuckle fighters! Good heavens, Drake, I never knew you were into that sort of thing … you mean thugs?
Drake	Yes, I suppose I do.
	Both laugh.
Metzler	Thank goodness for that – I thought you wanted *me* to go in and …
Drake	Now don't be ridiculous, Metzler.

Scene 8

Causing a scene at the Opera Comique, July 1879

The final performance of 'HMS Pinafore' is taking place at the Opera Comique theatre. It is the end of the performance. The cast are bowing and the audience applauding and cheering and call for encore! encore! George Grossmith steps forward in the role of Sir Joseph.

Music: 'When I Was A Lad'.

Sir joseph	When I was a lad I served a term
	As office boy to an attorney's firm.
	I cleaned the windows and I swept the floor,
	And I polished up the handle of the big front door.
	I polished up that handle so carefullee
	That now I am the Ruler of the Queen's Navee!
Chorus	He polished up that handle so carefullee
	That now he is the Ruler of the Queen's Navee!
Sir joseph	As office boy I made such a mark
	That they gave me the post of a junior clerk.
	I served the writs with a smile so bland,
	And I copied all the letters in a big round hand —
	I copied all the letters in a hand so free,
	That now I am the Ruler of the Queen's Navee!
Chorus	He copied all the letters in a hand so free,
	That now he is the Ruler of the Queen's Navee!

During Sir Joseph's verse we start to hear shouts off stage that build to a full scale fracas.

Stage crew — Hey you can't come in here. Who are you? Clear off. Go away. Get

	out, go on get out.
Thugs	No mate, you get out of our way. We're here to take the set.
Stage crew	Get out. It doesn't belong to you.
Thugs	It does now. So piss off and get out of our way.
Stage crew	Stop them. Stop them. Get 'im, Get 'im.
Thugs	We're taking it whether you like it or not.

George Grossmith steps forward above the noise and addresses the audience. The girls in the cast get involved and bash the thugs with whatever props there are to hand.

Grossmith	Ladies and gentlemen, please, please be calm. I assure you there is no reason to be alarmed. It seems some thugs have been hired by the directors of the Comedy Opera Company to steal the set of our show whilst Mr D'Oyly Carte is in the United States of America. However *(peers into the wings)*, it does appear that our valiant stage crew are defending our position gallantly and the police have been called.

Curtain

End of Act 1

Scene 9

The winter of discontent, February 1880

The scene is set during a rehearsal of 'Pirates of Penzance' which had its premiere in New York on 31st December 1879. Gilbert is pacing up and down looking concerned.
Suggested Music: Offstage SFX 'With Cat-Like Tread'.

Enter Jessie Bond.

Jessie	Mr Gilbert, may I have a word please.
Gilbert	Yes, yes of course Miss Bond. I hope your illness hasn't spoilt your first taste of New York.
Jessie	No, I am delighted to be here. I thought I'd be homesick, but it's much too exciting.
Gilbert	And how are you feeling now?
Jessie	I'm very much better thank you. It was so kind of Mr Sullivan to pay my doctor's bill – I really didn't know how I would be able to pay it.
Gilbert	Sullivan is a generous man. He's suffered greatly with his own health recently so he was sympathetic to your predicament. Before the opening night he was miserably ill with pain from his kidney problems, but he had to work until 5 am to finish the overture. He had four hours sleep, came to the theatre to rehearse the piece, went back to bed and then dined on champagne and a dozen oysters.
Jessie	He still got a standing ovation and nine encores.
Gilbert	*(Aside)* If he'd left the oysters he might have got a dozen encores.
Jessie	I hope you won't think me ungrateful, Mr Gilbert … but as you know I'm playing the part of Edith in the 'Pirates of Penzance' and …

Gilbert	Yes, my dear?
Jessie	Now that I am more experienced … and I know Mr Sullivan approves of my voice and I do have ambition, well … I was wondering if it might be possible that the part … be improved.
Gilbert	Oh. Oh I see. Hmmm … I could add some dialogue. *(Jessie looks pleased)* But it would be obvious padding and I don't see that it would do you any real good. *(Jessie looks disappointed)* But, I can tell you that we are already working on a new opera and I have written a much bigger part for you. Much bigger. *(Jessie looks pleased.)* My dear Jessie, I, indeed Mr Sullivan and I, have a very special regard for you. We would be most upset to lose you.
Jessie	I'm flattered, Mr Gilbert. I don't know what to say.
Gilbert	Nothing to say, my dear. Nothing to say. It's going to be a busy and exciting year. We have the London debut of 'Pirates' in a few weeks' time and our next opera is ….
	Enter Carte.
Carte	Good morning, I trust I'm not interrupting.
Jessie	Good morning, sir … I'm–
Carte	Just leaving?
Jessie	Yes, sir.
	Jessie exits.
Carte	Miss Bond is developing into a fine performer and she has a good character.
Gilbert	Yes, and I regard it as a duty to ensure that the young actresses in our company remain in good character, which means the company

	must be run on the lines of strict propriety.
Carte	Quite right, Gilbert.
Gilbert	We can't tolerate any loose word or gesture either behind the stage or on it.
Carte	It's the only way to shake off the bawdy image of musical theatre. We must have nothing vulgar or offensive.
Gilbert	Nothing offensive! Unless of course we're offending politicians and public servants.
Carte	Well as long as it doesn't harm the reviews. Do you realise tonight is the last performance of 'HMS Pinafore' in London – 571 performances.
Gilbert	Quite an achievement.
Carte	I think we've done rather well, and even better since we managed to shake off the Comedy Opera Company.
Gilbert	Hmmm.
Carte	You sound doubtful.
Gilbert	I have concerns.
Carte	Concerns? Why?
Gilbert	I seem to be fighting a constant battle with every production to get Sullivan to complete the score on time. He's always off hither and thither attending to his 'other interests' and on that subject I think his relationship with Mrs Fanny Ronalds is inappropriate.
Carte	They're longstanding friends. You can't deny him friendships.
Gilbert	Oh come on, Carte. You and I know perfectly well she is a great distraction from our enterprise and I know that when a man is greatly

	distracted there is usually a very good reason.
Carte	Nevertheless, he continues to write wonderful music that our audiences love. 'The Pirates of Penzance' has been running here in New York for seven weeks and you, Sullivan and I have *each* made more money every week than a working man in England earns in three years.
Gilbert	Each?
Carte	Yes, we share the profit three ways as per the agreement we drafted last June. Well, you drafted actually.
Gilbert	Yes, yes, I know that, but tell me Carte, *(pause)* what do you *do*? I mean what do you actually bring to the concern? In London, for example, all you have to do is look after the advertisements and sign contracts when performers are engaged. I estimate £20 a week would generously cover a good man to do those tasks.
Carte	What? I work from dawn till dusk to develop the opportunities for you and Sullivan.
Gilbert	But suppose Sullivan and I were to rent a theatre and employ a manager. It wouldn't cost a fraction of what we pay you.
Carte	I resent that, Gilbert. We share profits as agreed in our … your agreement. I have staked all I have in the world to build your reputations. Even now I have a legal action against me from the Comedy Opera Company that could bankrupt me.
Gilbert	But are you really comparing the creative skills of my libretti and Sullivan's music with your ability to talk fast and hire a theatre or two?
Carte	If it wasn't for my ideas and the creation of this new wave of musical theatre you would still be writing one-act plays and pantomimes. Do you seriously think that Arthur Sullivan would be interested in writing

	popular music for you, for which incidentally he is much criticised in the serious press, if it were not for the significant income my enterprise and hard work have given both of you?
Gilbert	I come up with the ideas, the plots, the setting, the characters, and I manage the rehearsals. All Sullivan has to do is to write the music … which he always leaves until the last minute and … for which he seems to get all the plaudits.
Carte	Let me tell you this, Gilbert, you need Sullivan, *we need* Sullivan and it is my work that keeps Sullivan in this business of ours. He's also very popular with Her Majesty the Queen and he's a personal friend of the Duke of Edinburgh, so I wouldn't be at all surprised if he doesn't become Sir Arthur Sullivan very soon. He's a professor at the Royal Academy of Music, he's principal of the National Training School for Music and he has no end of well-paid requests to work elsewhere.
Gilbert	Isn't it remarkable that he finds so much time for his gambling and womanising! It's no wonder he leaves everything until the last minute.
Carte	Rest assured, Gilbert, that I did not put myself in this position in order to relinquish my share of the profits or discuss the value of my services with you or anyone else. And whereas others have spent their reward I have reinvested the profits I have made. I have now completed the purchase of the old Savoy Palace site in the Strand and there I shall a build a magnificent theatre completely illuminated with electric lighting – the first anywhere in the world.
Gilbert	Hmmm, I look forward to seeing it, one day.
Carte	You won't have to wait long. I have already appointed the architect. My theatre will open next year and be a fitting venue for a new Gilbert

and Sullivan opera. I have risked everything on this, Gilbert, and I won't give up now.

Suggested music: 'The Major General's song' continues into scene 10.

Scene 10

Back home to Pirates, March 1880

Carte's office. He enters in a flurry.

Helen	Richard, you're back! It's so good to see you, welcome home.
Carte	Thank the Lord we are indeed safely home and to see you again, Helen!

Helen helps him off with his coat.

Helen	Was it difficult then, the New York crossing?
Carte	Choppy! A little like the whole expedition!
Helen	Oh dear. How successful do you think you've been in protecting the copyright for 'Pirates of Penzance' over there?
Carte	We just have to hope that our strategy worked, and if it doesn't then it won't be for lack of trying. We worked day and night to prevent the copycats from cheating us like they did with Pinafore.
Helen	I know, Richard, and it's taken its toll on all of you I fear.
Carte	Our plan to rehearse three or four companies at the same time to send out on tour was instrumental in forestalling the imitation productions. What with that, and having the original work produced and conducted by the creators themselves on US soil, New York would *not* this time be fobbed off with cheap substitutes.
Helen	Well you've put every effort into it.
Carte	Indeed, and every free moment we had was spent attending countless social functions to promote the thing!
Helen	Sounds exhilarating but exhausting … especially for Arthur no doubt.
Carte	Such a victim to his old trouble. The strain on him has been more

	evident I'm afraid. After one rehearsal I found him in a semi-comatose state from pain and overwork. You know how charming and pleasing he generally is, well I could tell he was getting close to the edge when he pronounced rather loudly to some socialite or other, that *'A free and independent American citizen ought not to be robbed of his right of robbing someone else!'*
Helen	Huh! I think that's the closest I've ever heard Arthur come to issuing an insult!
Carte	Indeed! Contrast that with Gilbert's riposte to some wealthy American woman at a fancy soiree when she announced that *'Mr Sullivan's music is really too delightful. It reminds me so much of dear Baytch.'*
Helen	Oh my word, did she mean Johann Sebastian?
Carte	Yes Bach the very same … *'Do tell me,'* she said, *'what is Baytch doing just now? Is he composing?'*
Helen	*(Laughs heartily.)*
Carte	'Well no, Madam,' Gilbert returned, 'just now as a matter of fact, Baytch is by way of decomposing'
	They both laugh.
Helen	Well I think congratulations are in order!
	A united front from the three of you sounds like it's gone a long way to stem the more voracious American theatre companies.
Carte	Well for all the effort we put in, I certainly hope so!
	It's been a very intense and exhausting experience I can tell you. I can't recall a time I've been more pleased to be back home.
Helen	Well we are all *very* pleased to see all of you back safe and sound.
	Though … I sense the discord between the partners is escalating.

Carte	Mmm … oh yes. You could well be right, but then you don't get more divergent temperaments than those two. It's hardly surprising.
Helen	Oh it's more than that, Richard.
Carte	Ohhh?
Helen	William is quite dominant, and Arthur's admiration of him has something of the, I don't know … feminine about it.
Carte	Feminine? Mmm … Well, as I see it, Gilbert brings out the best in Sullivan, though I confess at times he is a little overwhelmed by Gilbert … in awe even, on occasions.
Helen	Yes perhaps that's more like it …? William is a very awesome character and he seems able to get the light-hearted and happy side from Arthur in his music …

They both concur.

    … but there's more to it than what is otherwise an ideal partnership.

Carte	In what way?
Helen	I think William's jealous of the music he's inspired in Arthur …
Carte	… Who is in turn annoyed by his dependency on our librettist extraordinaire!
Helen	It was evident before, but I've become more aware of it even before your trip to the States. At first it was just banter from William and quiet reserve from Arthur but now …
Carte	Yes … it's really noticeable when Gilbert hears people whistling one of Sullivan's tunes. With no ear for music and little admiration for it, the constant repetition of those melodies (that would never have been written had it not been for his words), arouses …
Helen and Carte	*(Together)* … Resentment!

Carte	Quite! He sort of relieved himself of it in London by chaffing Sullivan in public, who, of course bore it quite patiently. But Gilbert's persistent facetiousness at the other's expense has definitely jarred with Sullivan whilst in New York.
Helen	And he is becoming bitter! Still, let's hope a big success for the London 'Pirates of Penzance' will take the sting away from Gilbert's lashing tongue.
Carte	Well they've no need to cross paths socially here, so they may be able to call a truce until 'Pirates' is in the bag!
Helen	Let's hope!
Carte	Now. How about some light refreshment and you can bring me up to date with what's happening here.

Suggested music: a few bars of 'Overture from The Pirates of Penzance'.

Scene 11

The Garrick Gentleman's Club, April 1880

Sullivan is seated with two whisky tumblers, a table and another chair.

Waiter	Mr Frederic Clay to see you, Mr Sullivan.
Sullivan	Fred, good to see you, old chap. I have your usual malt at the ready

Hands him a glass.

Fred Clay	Excellent, thank you, Arthur. Have you seen Gilbert since the 'Pirates' premiere?
Sullivan	Only out of necessity. I actually don't know how much longer I can put up with his continuous carping!
Clay	Oh come now, Arthur. I know it's trying. Gilbert has a sharp tongue and a wicked wit. Can you not recall the first time you two met? I introduced you of course and he instantly got the upper hand when he solicited your view about … *(impersonating Gilbert's pomposity)* 'The musical merits of the simple tetrachord of mercury, in which (as I need not tell you) there are no diatonic intervals at all, as upon the much more complicated dis-diapason (with the four tetrachords and the redundant note) which embraces in its perfect consonance all the simple, double and inverted chords?'

They both laugh heartily.

Sullivan	You committed it to memory … that's priceless!
Clay	I did! I've never heard anything so contrary and so funny. The man knows little to nothing about music and even less about its merits! It's inconceivable that you two should be friends such as we are, Arthur, but what a partnership you make!

Sullivan	The truth is, he doesn't much care for music. Gilbert always says he only knows two tunes. One is 'God Save the Queen' and the other one isn't.
Clay	You see my point.
Sullivan	I know, Fred … I shouldn't let it affect me so much. I know it's just banter from Gilbert but the joke is always at my expense.
Clay	How about calling some sort of truce … or at least a peace offering to Gilbert. See what he makes of it?
Sullivan	A gesture of friendship you mean?
Clay	Why not? One last attempt at a workable alliance.
Sullivan	Mmmm. There is one thing I might try and it just may be a way of hinting to Gilbert that in future he should supply me with more serious libretti. I suppose I could ask him to prepare a verse-version of the 'Martyr of Antioch' that I'm preparing for the Leeds Festival on the 15th October.
Clay	Good idea, Arthur … the perfect olive branch.

They clink glasses in a toast to the new idea.

Scene 12

Patience is a virtue, April 1881

Music: 'A Policeman's Lot'.

Gilbert is off stage watching.

When a felon's not engaged in his employment (his employment)
Or maturing his felonious little plans (little plans)
His capacity for innocent enjoyment (-cent enjoyment)
Is just as great as any honest man's (honest man's)

Our feelings we with difficulty smother (-culty smother)
When constabulary duty's to be done (to be done) ah,
Take one consideration with another (with another)
A policeman's lot is not a happy one ahhh

When constabulary duty's to be done,
To be done,
A policeman's lot is not a happy one (happy one).

When the enterprising burglars not a'burgling (not a'burgling)
When the cut throat isn't occupied in crime (-pied in crime)
He loves to hear the little brook a'gurgling (brook a'gurgling)
And listen to the merry village chime (village chime)

When the coster's finished jumping on his mother (on his mother)
He loves to lie a'basking in the sun (in the sun) ah,
Take one consideration with another (with another)
A policeman's lot is not a happy one ahhh

	When constabulary duty's to be done,
	To be done,
	A policeman's lot is not a happy one (happy one).
	Roars of applause and encores. Rutland Barrington bumps into Gilbert.
Barrington	Oh, Mr Gilbert! This happens every night now, sir. We can't move on with the show until we've had at least two verse encores every night. Twice! It occurs to me that you might write me an 'encore' verse. It would, I'm sure, add enormous popularity to the song.
Gilbert	Encore means sing it again, Barrington!
	He turns abruptly and walks away swiftly, bumping into Helen. Music continues low in the background as audience laugh and applaud.
Helen	'Pirates' is doing so well, William, isn't it!
Gilbert	Indeed it is, Helen, and I've made good progress working on its successor, 'Patience', after a somewhat shaky start.
Helen	What's the story, William?
Gilbert	I could see the way the wind was blowing with the Aesthetic craze in frenzy currently and was taken with adding a few puffs of my own.
Helen	Did you hear that Oscar Wilde was apparently seen in Piccadilly wearing what can only be described as fancy dress, and have you seen the stinging comments from the press? Just up your street, William.
Gilbert	Yes, but after everything that's happened in the last few months, I was struck by a fit of laziness and instead dabbled with an idea I had a while back in my satirical writing, 'The Rival Curates'.
Helen	Oh?
Gilbert	Curates are more absurd than Aesthetes don't you think? Anyhow,

	the Aesthetes have been lampooned sufficiently already in *Punch*. Besides, I really dislike the affectations of Parsons! And I hate the way they seem to be idolised by women!
Helen	Your objection to the clergy is legendary, William!
Gilbert	I did once find myself the only layman among a company of 'the divines' at a conference in the town where I was staying, one of whom addressed me with quiet irony; 'I should think, Mr Gilbert,' he said, 'you must feel slightly out of place in this company?' 'Yes,' I said, 'I feel like a lion in a den of Daniels!'
Helen	William, you are wicked!
Gilbert	So between laziness and inclination I began the libretto that would hold the typical curate up to ridicule. But, I hadn't worked on it for very long when I began to have severe twinges of caution.
Helen	Sounds most unlike you.
Gilbert	I had doubts about its popularity and wondered whether people would be amused by a chorus of comical curates, after all I wouldn't want our audiences to think I was laughing at religion now … and even with a devout composer of oratorios composing the music … No, it was too dangerous!
Helen	So you rather cleverly reverted to your original plan.
Gilbert	Yes, and I might say, with a sigh of relief, I went after safer game!
Helen	Well good luck with completion then, William, I can't wait to read it.
Gilbert	I've already given the first draft to Sullivan so it shouldn't be too long now. Goodnight, Helen.
Helen	Goodnight and give my best wishes to Lucy.
Gilbert	I will indeed.

He exits and Helen moves upstage where she meets with Sullivan.

Helen	Good evening, Arthur! May I just offer my congratulations on such a resounding success at Leeds Festival. You must be delighted. I've got the Leeds Mercury here as it happens *(she opens the newspaper)* 'The cheers which greeted the arrival of Mr Sullivan were renewed with still more vigour and enthusiasm at the close of his new work. The whole assemblage indeed joined in a heavy tribute!' Well done! The Princess of Wales must be thrilled with her dedication … what did she say? Do tell.
Sullivan	Oh well, you know. All I hear are grave questions as to how I reconcile writing a moving anthem like 'Brother thou hast gone before us' with setting music to such nonsense as 'When the enterprising burglar's not a burgling!'
	But there you are. I find myself post-Leeds somewhat reluctant to tackle lesser themes, so I have packed Gilbert's first draft of 'Patience' in a bag, dismissed the subject from my mind, and depart for the Riviera and Italy for a couple of months first thing tomorrow.
Helen	A couple of months, Arthur! Well, I'm sure it will do you good. Enjoy the sunshine and come back refreshed won't you.
Sullivan	I'm looking forward to the rest if I'm honest, but my ulterior motive is that there's also a rather interesting scheme I might invest in. To float a tramway company!
Helen	Oh, interesting. And will you be seeing the Duke of Edinburgh whilst on your travels? I hear he is with his squadron in the Baltic.
Sullivan	Who knows who one will bump into next! *(He starts to exit.)*
Helen	Be sure to give Mrs Rolands my best wishes won't you, Arthur?
Sullivan	Will do, Helen, will do. *(Walks off waving)* Au revoir!

Scene 13

Savoy small talk, October 1882

Suggested music: 'Tripping Hither, Tripping Thither'.

Jessie and George meet at the stage door of the Savoy Theatre, London.

Grossmith	Do you know anything about this new production, Jessie?
Jessie	Well, you know the title, George? 'Iolanthe'.
Grossmith	Yes, and it makes me think 'fairies'. Am I right?
Jessie	You are. *(Dances in fairy fashion)* I'm in the fairy chorus.
Grossmith	That won't please Mr Sullivan then. He'll be complaining again that he wants more serious libretti.
Jessie	But he will have composed some wonderful music. I can't wait to hear it today. Oh George, it's so exciting isn't it? 'Iolanthe' is the first comic opera to *actually premiere* at Mr D'Oyly Carte's Savoy Theatre, and you and I will be in it!
Grossmith	It is a wonderful theatre. I've played it since last year when we transferred here with 'Patience'. Very comfortable. No fumes or smells like we had with the old gas lamps. This electric lighting they've installed is amazing. I wouldn't be surprised if the whole country doesn't have it before long.
Jessie;	And it can provide what they're calling 'special effects'. Apparently, the fairy chorus have got electric sparkling magic wands. And there are telephones! The prompt desk can telephone the dressing rooms! Isn't that amazing?
Grossmith	It is indeed. It was a brilliant idea of Mr D'Oyly Carte's to build his own theatre with every possible modern amenity. I wonder if the two great

	men are speaking today or if there's been yet another falling out?
Jessie	Well, I have heard there have been a few squabbles …
Grossmith	Squabbles! Mr Gilbert was furious with Mr Sullivan for going abroad and missing a scheduled meeting.
Jessie	But poor Mr Sullivan's mother died in the summer. He was quite devoted to her. It hit him very hard and I expect it affected his health so badly he had to get away.
Grossmith	And Mr Carte and Mr Gilbert have had contractual differences over 'Iolanthe', and *(He pauses for dramatic effect)* about Frank Thornton's employment!
Jessie	*(Gasps)* Frank, your understudy? No! Is he still with the company?
Grossmith	Oh yes, Mr Carte wanted to give him a leading role, but Mr Gilbert insisted he stay as understudy.
Jessie	Oh dear, are they still at daggers drawn? Mr Gilbert won't tolerate any interference in his ideas for casting or for staging of any production.
Grossmith	I believe it was quite a heated discussion!
Jessie	Well, George, amidst all this conflict we must just be thankful that we have been employed again!
Grossmith	We won't be in anything, Jessie darling, if we stand here gossiping, Mr Gilbert will replace us in a twinkling if we're late! Come on … *(Exit.)*

Scene 14

Princess Ida's final performance, October 1884

Gilbert, Sullivan, Carte and Helen in wings of 'Princess Ida', Savoy Theatre, London, looking despondent.

Suggested music: Strains of 'If You Give Me Your Attention'.

Sullivan	*(Brightly, trying to be positive)* It might be Princess Ida's last evening, but 246 performances is hardly a failure. Hmm?
Helen	The long hot summer undoubtedly affected ticket sales. *(Silence as they all think.)*
Sullivan	On reflection, Gilbert's decisions to use blank verse, and have three acts instead of our usual two, might not have been wise. *(No one speaks, but Richard and Helen exchange concerned looks and Gilbert looks stony faced.)*
Sullivan	I also fear, Gilbert, that your decision to dismiss the sublime Lilian Russell from the title role was a great mistake. She undoubtedly would have attracted bigger audiences. You have done your best, of course, in staging the production but, sadly, you appear to have fallen short.
Gilbert	You would not, of course, blame the poor quality of the music, Sullivan!
Sullivan	How damnably rude. My apologies for my language, Helen dear. The critics praised my music as 'majestic' and described 'The World Is But A Broken Toy' as one of my most beautiful and plaintive melodies. *(Pompously)* I was favourably compared to the great Gounod! The failing is not mine, Gilbert! *(Gilbert snorts contemptuously.)*
Carte	This is no time for quarrelling, gentlemen! Sir Arthur, your music was

	as delightful as ever, and Mr Gilbert, I assure you, the libretto was good.
Gilbert	Good? Good? Why you, you administrator! Pray continue to administrate your curtains, carpets, privies and tickets, but spare me your pedestrian views. Your theatrical opinion is of no consequence whatsoever. You sir, are NOT AN ARTIST. *(Turns on his heel and exits.)*
Sullivan	Well really!
Helen	You must both stay calm. The production has not failed. The run has been respectably long, and indeed, has been lucrative. We all know what William is like. He has a fiery temperament but tomorrow he will be sorry for his words. Richard, no one else underestimates how hard you work to make these productions so successful, and Arthur, I think William is a little jealous of your wonderful musicality and your popularity with the public, perhaps even how highly the royal family regards you.
Carte	He'd never admit it, but I do believe Gilbert is jealous of your knighthood.
Helen	However, Arthur you were rather hard on William, but even so I am sure we shall all be reconciled and will work together again. You both still have many years of success ahead of you. Now come, let us go and speak to the cast and thank them for all their hard work.

Scene 15

The Mikado: rehearsal and rebellion, March 1885.

'Mikado' rehearsal. Gilbert and various artistes.

Suggested music: A few bars from 'Three Little Maids'.

Gilbert	Miss Bond, Miss Braham and Miss Grey, step forward please. Monsieur D'Auban has been instructing you, with the help of Miss Sixpence, from the Japanese Exhibition, is that not so?
Maids	Yes, Mr Gilbert.
Gilbert	Sir Arthur has given us a splendidly light tripping introduction on the strings and flutes, which perfectly sets the mood for the melody you are about to delight us with, dear ladies.
Maids	Yes, Mr Gilbert.
Gilbert	Despite your shuffling gait, wigs, Japanese make up and dresses, I require that the audience should immediately recognise you as English girls straight out of a Kensington ladies seminary. 'The Mikado' might be set in an exotic land but all the characters must act like English men and women. Do I make myself clear?
Maids	Yes, Mr Gilbert.
Gilbert	Have you been working on your fans, ladies?
Maids	Yes, Mr Gilbert.
Gilbert	Then let us see the results of your labours.

Maids snap fans open at different speeds.

Gilbert	Again, please

Maids snap fans open at different speeds.

Gilbert	Again, please and this time kindly synchronise a slow raising of the

	fan and a speedy flick of the wrist in a downward movement.
Leonora	Excuse me, Mr Gilbert
Gilbert	Yes, Miss Braham
Leonora	When you say synchronise, is it that you wish us all to raise and lower the fans at the same time?
Gilbert	Indeed, Miss Braham.
Leonora	So we are not to follow Monsieur D'Auban's previous instructions?
Gilbert	Indeed not, Miss Braham, if Monsieur D'Auban's previous instruction differs in any way to the clear and precise request I have just made to you, Miss Grey and Miss Bond, to synchronise a slow raising of the fan and a speedy flick of the wrist in a downward movement. Am I making myself understood?
Maids	Yes, Mr Gilbert.
Gilbert	Thank you, ladies, then once again, your fans please.
	Maids perform more or less together.
Gilbert	Better. And again.
	Maids perform together.
Gilbert	Better. And again.
	Maids perform together.
Gilbert	Excellent. The chorus will also synchronise this movement, that is to say, Miss Braham, they will also ignore any previous instructions from Monsieur D'Auban and each will perform a slow raising of the fan and a speedy flick of the wrist in a downward movement. All at the same time as each other and at the same time as you three ladies. Is that quite clear?
Maids	Yes, Mr Gilbert.

Gilbert	Now, I should like to continue and see the moves you have learned and the new use of the fans if you please. Music please!

Maids perform 'Three Little Maids' all verses. At end of song, member of cast rushes in and starts whispering to other cast members, cries of consternation.

Three little maids from school are we
Pert as a school-girl well can be
Filled to the brim with girlish glee
Three little maids from school

Eveything is a source of fun
Nobody's safe, for we care for none
Life is a joke that's just begun
Three little maids from school

Three little maids who, all unwary
Come from a ladies' seminary
Freed from its genius tutelary
Three little maids from school
Three little maids from school

One little maid is a bride, Yum - Yum
Two little maids in attendance come
Three little maids is the total sum
Three little maids from school
Three little maids from school

From three little maids take one away
Two little maids remain, and they
Won't have to wait very long, they say
Three little maids from school

>
> Three little maids from school
> Three little maids who, all unwary
> Come from a ladies' seminary
> Freed from its genius tutelary
> Three little maids from school
> Three little maids from school

Gilbert | *(Thunders)* **How dare you disrupt my rehearsal. This is intolerable.** *(He throws down his notes, and storms offstage. Cast gathers round to hear news.)*

1st Character | Mr Gilbert has upset Mr Temple. He has cut his only solo. Mr Temple is crying in the dressing room.

2nd Character | No!

1st Character | Yes – Mr Gilbert has cut 'My Object All Sublime'!

2nd Character | Oh no, Mr Temple has been working so hard on that despite all of Mr Gilbert's criticism and his pushing him to get it right.

1st Character | Mr Temple is extremely distressed. Sir Arthur is with him now.

2nd Character | Well, we must do something about it. The song is wonderful and Mr Temple sings it beautifully – now – let's get all the chorus together, and Jessie Bond and George. Someone must speak to Mr Gilbert and make him change his mind.

1st Character | Mr Gilbert??!!! CHANGE HIS MIND????!!!! Are you mad? He's never going to change his mind. Mr Gilbert's word is law. No one is allowed to challenge his direction – not even Sir Arthur or Mr D'Oyly Carte! He's certainly never going to listen to us.

3rd Character | Miss Lenoir! Miss Lenoir can make him change his mind! I'll get her.

2nd Character | Go and get everyone together *(Pushes other actor off stage and then calls after him)* and I'll get Mr Temple and Sir Arthur. *(Exits calling 'Mr*

Temple, Mr Temple', more chorus members begin to assemble, looking shocked and murmuring amongst themselves nervously, followed by Sullivan and Temple.)

2nd Character   Ah, Sir Arthur! Something must be done. Mr Gilbert must be persuaded to reinstate Mr Temple's solo. Will you speak on behalf of us all please? *(Cast all look at Sir Arthur).*

Sullivan   Er, no. I fear it would be pointless, a wild goose chase. I have no influence, or indeed any importance, in Mr Gilbert's artistic stronghold. I am a mere cipher.

Helen arrives hurriedly.

2nd Character   Miss Lenoir, should I fetch Mr Carte?

Helen   No, definitely not. I have to tell you that Mrs Carte, who, as you know, has been very ill for some time, has just, sadly, passed away. *(Shocked reaction from the cast and murmuring)* So we must leave Mr Carte and young Lucas and young Rupert to grieve. *(More murmurings and shocked looks)* Now, I've heard what's happened and I believe your best plan is to speak to Mr Gilbert yourselves. *(To 1st Character)* Please go and ask Mr Gilbert to meet us here. *(1st Character looks aghast, hesitates, is urged to go and reluctantly leaves)* Mr Temple you must explain to Mr Gilbert how hard you have worked on the song and assure him that you think it will be a great success. *(Temple, nods, tremulously tries to look brave, wrings hands)* We will all support you. *(Chorus nods and makes encouraging noises. Enter Gilbert, followed by 1st Character.)*

Gilbert   Well?

Silence. All look at Temple. He attempts to speak, gulps, then weeps, takes out handkerchief, waves it wordlessly. Gilbert turns to go. Consternation amongst the chorus. Helen pushes Jessie forward. They look at each other and Helen nods encouragingly.

Jessie Mr Gilbert? Mr Gilbert, it's very good of you to meet us, sir. We all know how tremendously busy you are. We're here because we've all heard of your decision to cut Mr Temple's solo *(She indicates Temple, whom the Chorus push forward. He again attempts to speak but breaks down).* It is, of course, solely your decision. Your artistic vision and control are legendary and your imaginative and dedicated staging of your work is always superb and has been supremely successful. *(Chorus nods enthusiastically)* We would not normally question your judgement, sir, as it is proven to be impeccable. However, on this occasion, might we suggest that the song is absolutely delightful, and you would be depriving our audiences of a real treat if you do not include it? Mr Temple so loves the music *(Chorus push him forward again, he tries to smile appealingly at Gilbert)* that he has worked extremely hard to hone it to your satisfaction, sir. It is ready for performance. We implore you to allow the public the chance to hear it. Do you think you might possibly be prevailed upon to include it on the opening night – just to test its appeal?

Pause. All, except Gilbert, hold their breath.

Gilbert Agreed.

Turns and walks off. Chorus turn to each other, laugh and exclaim and clap hands. Jessie looks stunned, Temple grabs her hands and kisses them. Sullivan throws hands in air and walks off. Temple moves joyously to front of stage and sings.

Temple A more human Mikado never
Did in Japan exist,
To nobody second,

I'm certainly reckoned,
A true philanthropist.
It is my very immune endeavour
To make, to some extent.
Each evil liver a running river
Of harmless merriment

Chorus.
My object all sublime
I shall achieve in time
To let the punishment fit the crime
The punishment fit the crime.
And make each prisoner pent
Unwillingly represent
A source of innocent merriment,
Of innocent merriment!

All prosy dull society sinners,
Who chatter and bleat, and bore,
Are sent to hear sermons
From mystical Germans
Who preach from ten to four.
The amateur tenor, whose vocal villainies
All desire to shirk,
Shall, during off-hours,
Exhibit his powers
To Madame Tussaud's wax work.

Chorus.
My object all sublime
I shall achieve in time-

To let the punishment fit the crime-
The punishment fit the crime..
And make each prisoner pent
Unwillingly represent
A source of innocent merriment,
Of innocent merriment!

Scene 16

The carpet quarrel, December 1889.

Carte is seated at desk working on papers. Helen is reading correspondence. An agitated Gilbert enters, waving papers which he thumps down in front of Carte.

Carte	*(Patiently puts down pen and greets Gilbert courteously)* Good morning, Gilbert.
Gilbert	Your letter is insulting, Carte! I demanded an explanation for staggeringly high levels of expenditure on your part, and you reply by accusing me of perpetual interference in matters that do not concern me, and write that you and Sullivan will have to look for another librettist! You have some explaining to do, Carte. This *(Hammers on papers on desk)* is fraud!
Carte	How dare you!
Gilbert	How dare I? How dare I? I, sir, do not dare to defraud my colleagues – as do you. These accounts are as much a work of fiction as the plot of 'The Pirates of Penzance'!
Carte	Take care, Gilbert, you slander me.
Gilbert	Better to slander, than to steal!
Helen	William!
Gilbert	Helen, dear Helen. I do not include you in this accusation. Your integrity is beyond question, unlike your thieving new husband.
Carte	I have not stolen a penny from you!
Gilbert	No, far more than a penny. You charge the preliminary expenses of 'Gondoliers' at a stupendous £4,500 and include £500 for front-of-house carpets?

	How, sir, are Sir Arthur and I liable to pay £500 to recarpet *your* theatre? You are a cheat and a bounder.
Carte	May I remind you, Gilbert, that our contract quite properly allows me to charge for 'repairs incidental to the performance'.
Gilbert	New carpets for the front of the house cannot possibly be called 'repairs incidental to the performance'. You may as well stretch that to include everything belonging to the theatre, whether in the lobbies, staircases, auditorium or stage.
Carte	These are *preliminary* figures, I believe the more likely cost will be around £140.
Gilbert	Then, sir, you have at best made a serious blunder in the accounts, or at worst a deliberate attempt to swindle.
Carte	May I remind you that in these years of our partnership I have paid you more than £90,000 for your share of the profits of our productions?
Gilbert	So you too will have received that figure and probably more if your dubious accounting system is anything to go by. Not bad is it, Carte? Near £100,000, gained – I can't say earned – by the efforts of others? You are simply the tradesman who sells *my* creations of art! What? What? *(Sullivan enters during this speech.)*
Helen	You are grossly impolite, William. You address my husband in a way that I should not have thought you would have used to an offending menial!
Sullivan	Heavens above! What is going on here?
Carte	Gilbert has uttered the most foul calumnies against me.
Gilbert	Carte is a thief.

Helen	Come, come gentlemen, let us not quarrel. Surely this is simply a misunderstanding.
Sullivan	We have all been working extremely hard, and tensions and difficulties are bound to arise. Gilbert, I fancy you are overtired. Sit down, and let us discuss this properly without shouting and wild accusations.
Gilbert	You sound unbiased, Sullivan, but you will run to Carte's side, won't you, because he is to produce your proposed 'Grand Opera' at the Royal English Opera House. Not to mention how much you resent my complete artistic control at the Savoy. Well let me tell you that MY artistic control has been the keynote of our success.
Sullivan	We have been *equal* partners in D'Oyly Carte, Gilbert, since we pledged our first £1,000 each seven years ago!
Carte	Gilbert thinks I will charge you £500 for a new carpet, but in fact the figure is more like to be £140.
Sullivan	£140! Should we three fall out over such a paltry sum, my friend?
Gilbert	That 'paltry sum', Sullivan, represents financial impropriety. I do not trust him and will not work with him again.
Sullivan	Come, come, let us sit down and thrash this out until we are in accord again. *(Looks at Gilbert)* We two have had our differences have we not? I have argued for a change of direction away from topsyturvydom and mechanical plots. A compromise was reached, and the result was 'The Mikado'!
Gilbert	I have never questioned your probity, nor you mine. This man is a charlatan. The cost of the carpet is only one of the items to which I take exception.
Sullivan	Now, Carte, will you look at the accounts again old fellow, and

	consider adjusting anything under dispute by Gilbert?
Carte	After I have been vilified and wrongfully accused in the most aggressive and insulting manner? I most certainly will not! I will tolerate Mr Gilbert's presence in my office no longer, neither, sir, will you write for me and the Savoy ever again. Please leave immediately.
Helen	Richard, no!
Gilbert	I leave, Carte, but this business does not end here. I go straight to my solicitor to bring proceedings against you. You will rapidly learn that it is a mistake to kick down the ladder by which you have risen! *(Exits.)*
Helen	Richard – did you really write to William saying that you and Arthur will seek another librettist?
Sullivan	Carte, that was most improper and designed to be inflammatory.
Carte	I have grown excessively tired of his constant carping. He gives no value to the work that I, and Helen, carry out for the business and promotional side of our productions. He is brilliant at what he does, Sullivan, but so are you and so are we! It is a fair division of labour and we are all significant factors in our success.
Sullivan	He is also excessively litigious! He will carry out his threat to sue.
Carte	He may certainly do so.
Helen	Arthur … can you do something?
Sullivan	I will go to him, dear lady. But not for a few days. He needs to calm down and reflect. Don't attempt to contact him in the meantime, Carte.
Carte	Believe me, Sullivan, I have no such intention! I never wish to speak to him again, let alone work with him.

Scene 17

Finale

Gilbert, Sullivan, Carte and Helen are each seated on chairs in a line. Grossmith and Jessie are standing with them on stage. Chorus in background. Music to 'I've Got A Little List' begins. Grossmith and Jessie smile at each other and begin singing. During the song the two singers approach and move to indicate the other four characters as appropriate to the words, sing over their shoulders, and act at them and with each other. The four characters remain static and unresponding throughout.

Music: 'I've Got A Little List'

George & Jessie	As some day it may happen
	That an ending may be found
	We've got a little list
	We've got a little list
	Of society composers
	Who no longer are around
	But always will be missed
	But always will be missed
	Aimed at Gilbert:
	The lyricist conceptualist who insists that all obey
	Or else he could be suing at the very end of day
	His cutting tongue directed at those he must rehearse
	His temper running rampant getting louder and much worse
	But William was also kind and fun, his memory will persist
	And always he'll be missed
	Yes, always he'll be missed
Chorus	We've got him on the list – we've got him on the list
	So always he'll be missed, yes always he'll be missed.

George & Jessie	*Aimed at Sullivan:*
	Here's a man who loved the women, his gambling and his Queen
	The piano-organist – we've got him on the list!
	He yearned to be remembered as serious and supreme
	Oh how he will be missed, how sorely he'll be missed
	He didn't like the quarrels of Gilbert and D'Oyly Carte
	But loved society parties, and the flattery of his art
	He sailed the Riviera and sojourned in the East
	Where kings and maharajahs invited him to feast
	That singular anomaly – the musicologist
	Oh how he will be missed, how sorely he'll be missed!
Chorus	We've got him on the list – we've got him on the list
	So always he'll be missed, yes always he'll be missed.
George & Jessie	*Aimed at Carte:*
	Now here's a man of business, of finance, and hard of heart
	He's no philanthropist – we've got him on the list
	He's keen to make a bob or two, unswerving Mr Carte
	Who always will be missed, who always will be missed
	He built his own theatre – and found the wealthy backers
	Then gathered in the profits – and added up the ackers
	He built hotels, theatres too, to standards top and lofty
	A money man of vision, slightly tricky, but so oft he
	Was the singular anomaly, the mighty capitalist
	So yes he will be missed, oh yes he will be missed.
Chorus	We've got him on the list – we've got him on the list
	So always he'll be missed, yes always he'll be missed.
George & Jessie	*Aimed at Helen:*
	And here's the brilliant Helen, who's dearly loved by all
	Expert statistist – we've got her on the list
	Efficient and caring, she could sort out every squall

	She'll definitely be missed, yes definitely missed
	From contracts to the casting and every small detail
	She nursed and soothed and comforted
	Whilst sorting out the mail
	A teacher of mathematics, speaking fluent French
	Pouring oil on troubled waters with pluck you couldn't quench
	She's that singular anomaly the early feminist
	And how she will be missed, so very dearly missed
Chorus	We've got her on the list – we've got her on the list
	So always she'll be missed, yes always she'll be missed.
George & Jessie	*Aimed at audience:*
	There's the lyricist, musician and impresario
	And the lady that he kissed – they'll all of them be missed
	There was a nasty quarrel and twas downhill after that
	The glory days were over cos of that almighty spat
	Sir Arthur was the first to die, his health had suffered badly
	After him twas D'Oyly Carte, whose widow missed him sadly
	Gilbert, who'd been knighted, died whilst rescuing a swimmer
	Leaving the comic opera world very much the dimmer
	Helen was the last to pass, the loyal activist
	They're all of them on the list, they're all of them on the list
Chorus	We've got them on the list – We've got them on the list
	So they'll all of them be missed, yes they'll all of them be missed!

END

www.ingramcontent.com/pod-product-compliance
Ingram Content Group UK Ltd.
Pitfield, Milton Keynes, MK11 3LW, UK
UKHW051253180426
11947UKWH00020B/1691